Discus

Dr. Herbert R. Axelrod & Bernd Degen

Ultimately, discus varieties will have been sufficiently inbred so the color and form of the offspring of a genetically known pair will be uniform and predictable. This is the best quality spawn possible in 1990 from parents which look similar to the offspring. Initially these 4-month-old fish may appear similar, but if you look at the thickness of the red lines, as well as the overall color patterns, you will find that each individual is different.

The Allure of Discus

Dr. Herbert R. Axelrod & Bernd Degen
Photos by Fumitoshi Mori & others

Discus varieties or hybrids are available in several shapes and colors. Recently, since 1988, fixed strains with metallic pigments have been developed such as this light metallic blue derivative of *Symphysodon aequifasciata aequifasciata*, the green discus from Tefé.

Published by T.F.H. Publications, Inc.,
1 TFH Plaza, P.O.Box 427, Neptune City, New Jersey,
USA.

Typeset, designed, printed and bound in Neptune City,
N.J. USA by T.F.H. Publications, Inc.

Distributed world-wide in petshops specializing in
aquarium fishes.

*Dedicated to
Robine, Willi and
Adolfo Schwartz
for all they have done to bring
millions of Discus
safely out of the jungle.*

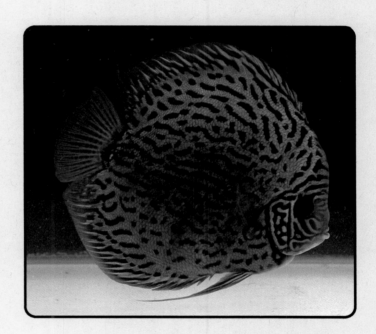

TABLE OF CONTENTS

This scribbled hi-fin is less than
a year old. It was developed in
Singapore and resulted from
several crosses between
*Symphysodon aequifasciata
haraldi* from the Purus River in
Brazil and *Symphysodon
aequifasciata aequifasciata*
from the Tefé lake region. This
type of fish is called 'fully
colored.'

This magnificent specimen of a hybrid *aequifasciata* is called a 'rainbow scribbled discus.' However, breeders and wholesalers give their fancy discus equally fancy names. If you are truly interested in reliable discus, ask to see a tankful of discus all of which should be very similar. Only this demonstration can prove that a strain is true breeding, thus making the offspring much more valuable.

AS THEY OCCUR IN THE WILD
Dr. Herbert R. Axelrod

For some reason, probably that of commercial secrecy, the exact locations of the collecting sites of many discus species and subspecies are erroneously reported in many books. Besides the desire to keep the specific locations of some species a secret, many writers on discus have never collected discus themselves. Other writers reporting on collecting trips may have found a few discus here and there, but in almost all of these cases the fishes were brought to the "collectors" by local fishermen. The local fishermen hold their fishing areas sacred and would never share their best spots with anyone else. The same is probably true of coldwater game fishermen who have their favorite fishing spots which they zealously guard as their personal secret.

From 1954-1974 I collected many discusfish in Lago Tefé, all of which looked very similar. I brought 32 back alive, giving the ones that died to Dr. Leonard P. Schultz , the Curator of Fishes at the United States National Museum, Smithsonian Institution, Washington, D.C., for further study. I also gave living specimens to such breeders as Dr. Edward Schmidt-Focke and commercial breeders in Florida. This shipment of discusfish became the basis of commercial discus breeding. Later on I collected blue discus in the Tefé River, as shown on the bottom of the facing page. Both of these photos were made on the spot. They have lost a lot of the color on the bodies of the fish because of the poor film and cameras available for use in the jungle when I found these fish in Tefé.

Hybrids produced from inbreeding selected specimens of *Symphysodon aequifasciata aequifasciata* and *Symphysodon aequifasciata haraldi*. These were the first outstanding specimens developed in Germany in 1980.

The result of this is that many writers rely upon other writers for distribution and range information and the errors become compounded.

The information I am presenting here is based upon my own personal knowledge. I have collected every species and every subspecies of discus in their natural habitats. Of course there are probably other areas in which these same (or other as yet undescribed species) discus may be found. But the hybrid color varieties on the market today have all been derived from the species I have collected since 1947. I don't intend to say that every discus used by the early discus hybridizers was collected by me personally. What I mean is that since I collected every species and subspecies, they had to use the same discus as their base stock.

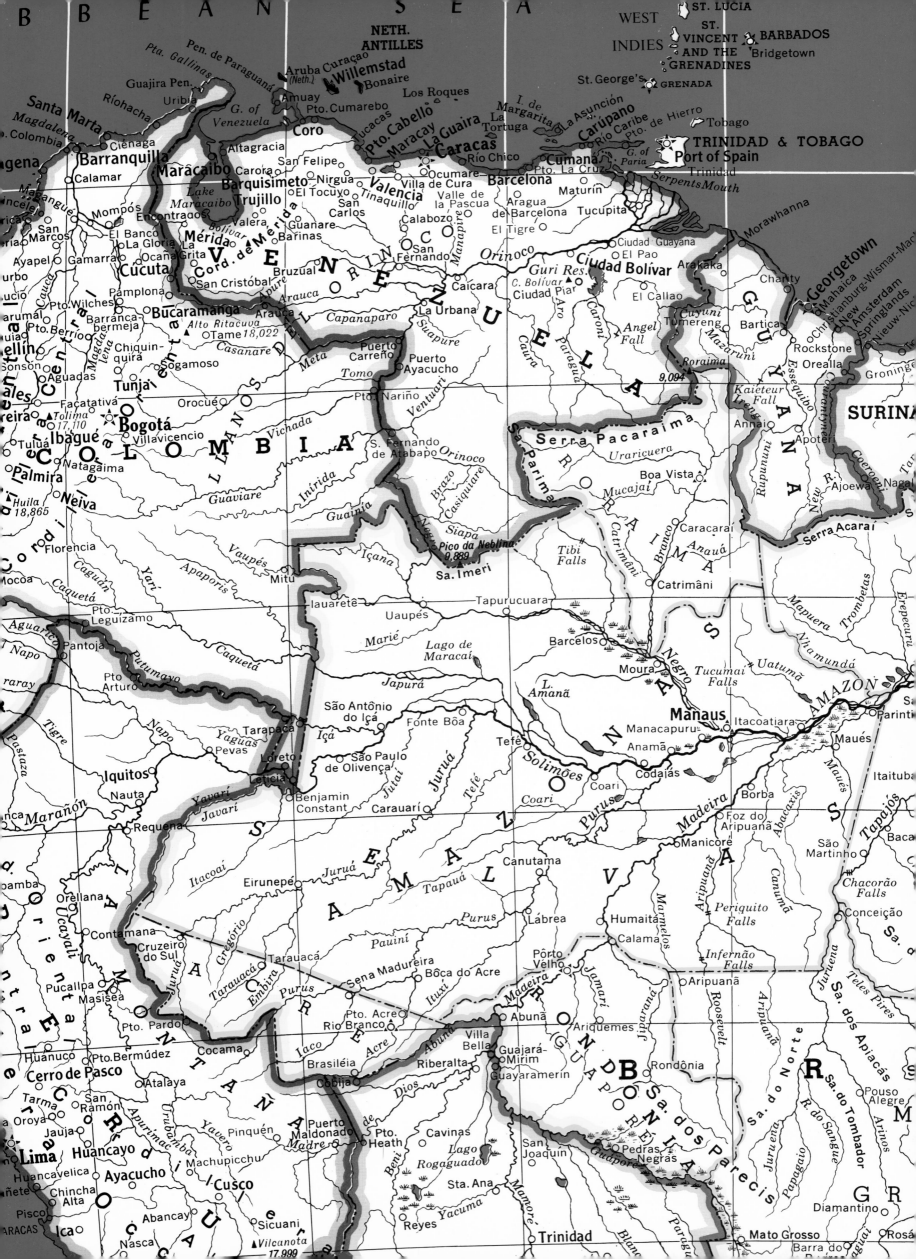

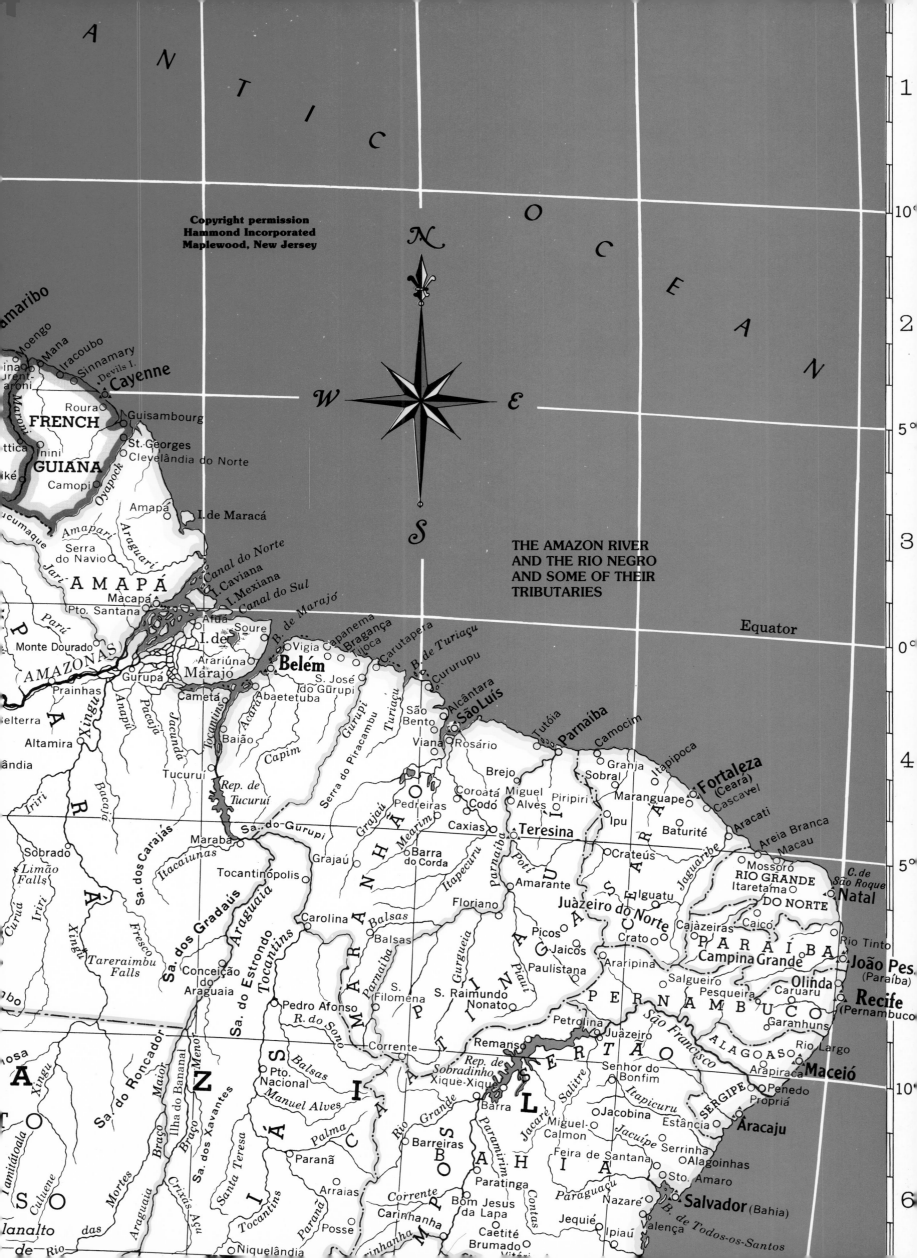

THE AMAZON RIVER
AND THE RIO NEGRO
AND SOME OF THEIR
TRIBUTARIES

I collected this highly colored female *Symphysodon aequifasciata aequifasciata* in the Rio Tefé. By
bringing back a few hundred living specimens and
judiciously giving them to breeders (free of charge,
by the way), intensely colored individuals developed from crossing various natural varieties of
Symphysodon aequifasciata. This was probably a
manifestation of the so-called 'hybrid vigor' which
often results in closely related inbred subspecies
being used for reproduction purposes.

CLASSIFICATION OF THE FISHES IN THE GENUS *SYMPHYSODON*.

In 1952 I had a wholesale fish com-
pany in New York called *World-wide
Aquarium*. We specialized in rare fishes.
In order to break the monopoly that the
Germans, Messrs. Schnelle and Cochu
and their firm Paramount Aquarium,
had on discus, I had to find a route from
the Amazon that did not pass through
Belem do Para, Brazil. In Belem the
Goeldi Museum, also dominated by
Germans, had granted Paramount the
sole and exclusive license to take fishes
from Brazil. Any other fishes coming
through Belem were confiscated and
turned over to Paramount.

From the blue form of *Symphysodon aequifasciata aequifasciata*,
shown above, intensive inbreeding done on a selective basis has
produced a solid blue high body
(hi-form in the trade), hi-fin discus. These fish were produced in
Southeast Asia, mainly Singapore.

Symphysodon discus discus Heckel from the Rio Jaú, a tributary running from the west into the Rio Negro. This variety was called the 'blue head' or 'cabeça azul'. These are photos taken immediately after I collected them. In actuality the fish are tremendously more colorful than shown here.

In searching for a new route from the Rio Negro port of Manaus to New York, I started in Manaus, Amazonas, Brazil. This was a sleepy little town of 20,000 people in those times. It has a legendary opera house which attested to the town's prominence during the rubber boom of the 1800's. At the time I was there it had no paved roads, no cars...nothing. I chartered a boat called *Barão de Madeira* and headed up the Rio Negro. I started collecting what was then called Discus Heckel, or the original *Symphysodon discus*, in small igarapes in just about every river system running off the Rio Negro including the Rio Jaú, Rio Unini (which was very rocky and was a different habitat for the discus), the Cuiuni, the Uneiuxi, the Marie and the Uapes. Igarapes, by the way, are barely navigable streams. All of the discusfish I found there were the original *Symphysodon discus* Heckel, 1840, a species with the three prominent broad bars on the sides. Many had slightly different colorations, but not different patterns.

Symphysodon discus discus Heckel from the Rio Negro. This is a wild fish.

12

Manaus, the capital of the state of Amazonas, Brazil is legendary. It was the rubber capital of the world more than 100 years ago, and one of the centers of culture in South America. The magnificent opera house still stands, having been rebuilt in 1988. Willi Schwartz, the discus king, had his home directly across the street from the opera house.

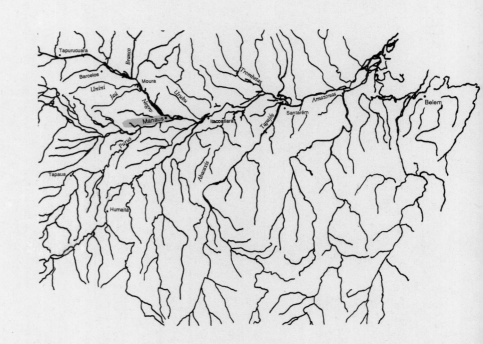

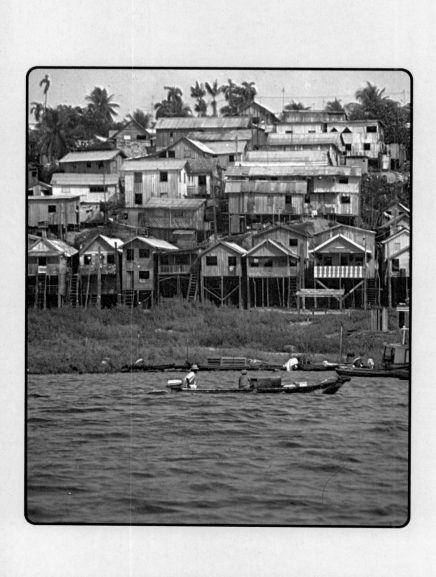

Modern Manaus is still fairly primitive for the poor people. The shacks have neither water, electricity nor sewer systems. The raw sewerage, though, has enriched the water and made it more suitable for maintaining a good food chain. It doesn't do much for the health of the people drinking it and swimming in it, though.

These are neon tetras, *Paracheirodon (Hyphessobrycon) innesi*. I thought I found giant neon tetras in the Rio Negro when I found the discus. I was wrong. The fish I found were a new species called *Cheirodon axelrodi*. They were named for me by Dr. Leonard P. Schultz.

While searching for discus in this area, I also found what I thought at the time were giant neon tetras, then *Hyphesso-brycon innesi*, but these later turned out to be a new species, the cardinal tetra, which was named in my honor as *Cheirodon axelrodi*. Since I was in business at that time (though still teaching at New York University), I became as interested in bringing these giant neons back alive as I was in bringing out discusfish. The only way out was to take the boat up the Rio Branco to the main city of Boa Vista, and then to charter a plane from Boa Vista to Georgetown, British Guiana (now called Guyana). The first time I tried this was a disaster.

These are cardinal tetras. They are the most popular of imported wild fishes. Many millions are imported every year and at prices which discourage breeding them commercially. Almosy 38 years ago, I sold them for $1.00 each. That dollar is probably worth $5.00 today. Yet the price in 1990, delivered in Miami, Florida, was 12¢ each.

The blue form of *Symphysodon aequifasciata aequifasciata* from the Tefé area. The discusfish from Tefé are very variable, obviously still going through evolutionary changes due to changes in their environment. By comparing the forehead stripes of red versus blue, you can have some idea of how much blue is on the body. Most of the color was scraped off during the storage of the fish in shallow containers during the night. I had to await the 10 a.m. sunlight to photograph these fish.

Arriving by boat in Boa Vista with the fishes was easy. The Rio Branco was wide and deep and we had no problems. It took a few days to arrange an airplane charter, so I started to change the water on the discus and cardinals. Within a day all died. The pH of the Rio Negro water was close to 3.0 while the Rio Branco was almost a neutral 7.0. The fishes could not tolerate this type of drastic pH change! I took the *Barão de Madeira* back down stream (the Rio Branco runs into the Rio Negro) and collected cardinals and discus all over again.

How comfortable it was collecting in the Rio Negro. The water is so acid that mosquitos cannot lay their eggs in it! The Rio Branco, on the other hand, is covered with swarms of mosquitos, making it very uncomfortable to work there.

An aerial view of the Rio Negro. In some cases the Rio Negro is miles wide without islands, but as you leave its junction with the Amazon, the Rio Negro looks more and more like this. The lower archipelago is the Anavilhanas. The upper one, which begins about the Rio Branco at Carvoeira and extends past Barcelos to the Demini and further to Tapurucuara, has not been officially named as yet.

This time, everything went along very well. Finally, a few weeks later, the fishes arrived with me in New York. The trip was so financially rewarding that at the age of 25 I was essentially set for life! In 1953 I was able to sell cardinal tetras for $1 each!

Having found a way out of Brazil that was not controlled by Paramount, I became more and more ambitious, and started to bring large quantities of discus and other fishes out of Brazil via Georgetown. This created a large business for Georgetown as Guyana itself had many desirable aquarium fishes like *Corydoras, Hypostomus,* gold tetras, hatchetfishes, *Anostomus,* and many others....but no discus or cardinals. So I began selling cardinals and discus to the Georgetown tropical fish exporters and thus the huge trade in South American fishes began.

17

A famous Singapore breeder, Gan Khian Tiong, supplied photographs of this strain through Dr. Clifford Chan. This is the highly prized scribbled blue, fully colored turquoise form. However, the background is obviously a marine aquarium. Discus could not live in such an aquarium. Either a photo tank was placed in front of a marine tank, or a print of the marine tank was used as a background for the photo tank.

18

As we catch the discus at night, we use a 'runner' who brings the discus to a floating net. If we keep the discus too long in 2 inches of water they injure themselves.

An ideal place to search for new fishes is a small stream of crystal clear spring water. This stream has lovely aquatic plants and lots of cardinal tetras, *Paracheirodon axelrodi*. The stream empties into the Rio Negro which is much more highly acid and contains no aquatic vegetation.

In 1956 I had already collected four distinctly different discusfish, all with different colors and color patterns. I showed color photographs of these fishes to Dr. Leonard P. Schultz who was, at that time, Curator of Fishes at the United States National Museum, Smithsonian Institution. He asked for specimens and in June, 1960, reviewed (in *Tropical Fish Hobbyist* magazine) the entire genus *Symphysodon*. The color photographs I sent were of living fishes I had collected. I took the photos within hours of catching the fishes and then preserved the discus. It was these specimens and photographs that I sent to Dr. Schultz. There are no photographs more scientifically valuable than those of living fishes that are then studied and subsequently described as new species or subspecies. Thus the photographs shown here cannot be duplicated. They are the most authentic, though far from the most beautiful, of the species. In 1953 there were very few color films available and they all had very slow speeds and short shelf-lives.

So I am presenting the original color photos plus color photos of the offspring of these wild discusfish.

20

The blue discus from Rio Tefé shown above was crossed with normal *Symphysodon discus discus* from the Rio Negro and produced (after 10 years of intensive selective breeding) the light blue or powder blue scribbled discus shown below.

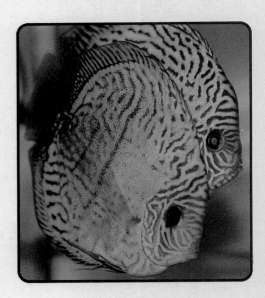

The red scribbled discus was produced without genes from *Symphysodon discus*. It contains only *Symphysodon aequifascata* genes.

When the Rio Tefé blue color variety shown on the facing page was crossed with the *Symphysodon discus discus* from Lago Batata, Rio Trombetas, this magnificent color hybrid was produced in Germany in 1980.

To catch discus in quantity we circle a tree which has fallen into the water and in which we have seen discus the night before. Then we chop up the tree, bit by bit, until there is nothing left of it. Then we pull in the seine. The discus are trapped. We move the seine to shallow water and put floats all around the edges. Then we remove the discus one at a time, by hand.

In the old days of the 1950-60's, when the boat *Ebenezer* was still young, we carried discus and cardinals in 5 gallon gasoline tins. The tops were cut open and folded back. The water was constantly siphoned out and fresh river water added. The trip from discus country in the Rio Negro to Manaus was three days and nights of constant travel.

Wild discus from the Rio Negro in Brazil. Most of them are practically identical as far as the numbers of scale rows, fin rays and body proportions, yet each has slightly different color patterns. Most wild discus are easily frightened, and this is evidenced in a lack of color. Even the broad, dark middle band is not too evident. Before fish like this can be bred, they must be tamed so they are comfortable with people moving around them and with the confines of an aquarium. Needless to say, *Symphysodon discus discus* Heckel should be kept in acid water. The pH of the Rio Negro varies from about 3.5 to 6.0. It is also dark in color. The closer you come to a dark water (your petshop has extracts or you can soak dry oak leaves) with a pH of about 5.2, the more comfortable will be your discus from the Rio Negro.

Wild discus from the Rio Negro are tamed and handfed by Bernd Degen before he attempts to breed them. He prefers to start with young fish about 4 inches in diameter. He handfeeds them until they begin to pair up by themselves.

25

DR. SCHULTZ'S REVIEW OF THE GENUS *SYMPHYSODON*, INCLUDING AN ADDITIONAL SUBSPECIES DESCRIBED BY DR. WARREN E. BURGESS.

The genus *Symphysodon* was first described by Heckel in 1840. The type species was named *Symphysodon discus* Heckel. The original description was published in the *Annals of the Vienna Museum (Ann. Wiener Museum)*, volume 2, page 332. All *Symphysodon* have ctenoid scales in vertical rows from the rear of the head to the base of the tail fin rays. The number of rows varies from 44 to 61, depending upon the species and subspecies. They all have nine vertical dark bars on the body including the head.

A wild discus, domesticated and handfed, in full color. This fish was collected from the Rio Negro by Adolfo Schwartz. This fish was originally in pretty poor condition when Schwartz collected it, as shown on the facing page. It takes months for the fish to become tame and regain their full health and vigor and lose their fear of being kept in an aquarium.

Adolfo Schwartz examines *Symphysodon discus discus* being offered to him by locals on the Rio Negro. The discus are transported in very shallow water in a plastic fish box. They are always in unfit condition when Schwartz buys them. They require a few weeks of good food, medication and rest before they can be sent on to Miami and from there all around the world.

Symphysodon discus
discus from the Rio
Negro are similarly
colored. They reproduce
very true to form as can
be seen by the small fish
in the center of the
group.

Symphysodon discus Heckel

The first species, *S. discus*, has 44 to 48
vertical rows in a straight line from the
rear of the head to the midbase of the
caudal fin rays. It is immediately distin-
guishable from the other species by
having three intensively colored,
broader bars. These are bars numbered
one, five, and nine. Different color varieties have more or less intense coloration
and prominence of these three bars and
the color of the background. Certain
individuals within the same population
are much more colorful than others, and
skillful breeders have been able to produce very beautiful specimens by inbreeding these highly colored individuals.

The original, wild, common *Symphysodon discus discus* from the Rio Negro of Brazil.

Wild *Symphysodon discus discus* from the
Rio Negro all have the same appearance in
the home aquarium. Their colors are
subdued and faded and they are never quite
at home. They lurk close to cover and shy
away from light.

By selective inbreeding of brother to sister from original wild parents of *Symphysodon discus discus* from the Rio Negro, magnificently colorful discus may be developed. This German jewel was produced about 1987.

Guarding the bluehead discus, *cabeça azul* as the indians call it, is this solitary indian house. It is built on high ground since the water has a mean rise of 18 feet between high and low water. The rainy season begins in December in the Rio Jaú, Brazil.

During the dry season, the normal habitat of *Symphysodon discus discus*, the blue-head, is exposed to view. When it rains, the water quickly rises in the Rio Jaú to cover the roots, and the discus spawn among these roots. We catch the discus among the roots at night with a strong light and a long-handled dip net.

An inbred strain of discusfish derived from *Symphysodon discus discus* from the Rio Negro. The fish on the facing page is a typical wild fish from the Rio Negro.

42

A wild *Symphysodon discus discus* from the Rio Negro, imported into Europe (where this photo was taken) more than 50 years ago.

44

The great mystery fish. Obviously this fish was produced by crossing a brown discus, *Symphysodon aequifasciata axelrodi*, with a Rio Negro discus, *Symphysodon discus discus*. Very few of these fish are ever seen on the market. They are very valuable.

The larger fish is a wild *Symphysodon discus discus* from the Rio Negro. The smaller fish, a female, is a *Symphysodon aequifasciata haraldi*. Crossing these fish is very common because the offspring are so varied.

45

The bluehead discus, or cabeça azul, which I found in the Rio Jaú and Rio Unini. Dr. Warren E. Burgess verified that they are almost identical to other Rio Negro discusfishes and do not deserve another scientific name. They are, however, highly prized for the production of new color varieties. Since the Rio Unini and Rio Jaú have been reserved as wildlife preserves, it is doubtful that many will find their way to aquariums. Only the few dozen families which live along these two rivers are allowed to fish for these discus.

On the sacred river, Rio Unini, discus collecting is forbidden. This area has been declared a reservation and no one is allowed in without special permission. The indians use this river to bury their dead because the river only rises a few feet each year and the cemetery is secure. I was astonished at the cleanliness of the cemetery...later I learned that there are three full time caretakers. It is the job of the three oldest ladies of the village. They usually live to the ripe old age of 40!

48

The real fish collectors are the indians. They know about every fish and every other living animal in their hunting area, even the smallest of fishes. When I write about the fishes 'I found,' it would be more honest if I wrote about the 'indian I found who took me to the fishes which were new to science.'

Symphysodon aequifasciata Pellegrin

In 1903 Pellegrin described fishes from Lago Tefé and Santarem as *Symphysodon discus aequifasciata*. The distance, by water, from Tefé to Santarem is at least 500 miles. Dr. Leonard P. Schultz examined about 100 specimens from Lago Tefé which I collected with Harald Schultz. He also examined discus I collected in the Belem do Para area and Benjamin Constant. These are perhaps 1,500 miles apart. Thus Dr. Schultz compared specimens of discusfishes from eastern to western Brazil, along the Amazon River. He concluded that Pellegrin's *Symphysodon discus aequifasciata* was a true species and not a subspecies, and that the fishes from the eastern, central and western parts of the Amazon River differ enough in coloration that they can easily be distinguished one from the others. Thus the species *Symphysodon aequifasciata* is further split into three subspecies namely *S. a. aequifasciata*, *S. a. axelrodi* and *S. a. haraldi*.

The green discus from the Rio Purus. It was named *Symphysodon aequifasciata haraldi* by Dr. Leonard P. Schultz. It honored Harald Schultz, who was not a relative of Dr. L. P. Schultz.

49

The green discus from the Tefé area. This is known scientifically as *Symphysodon aequifasciata aequifasciata*.

Symphysodon aequifasciata aequifasciata Pellegrin

This subspecies is found around Lago Tefé, a tributary of the Amazon River in Brazil. It is referred to as the "green discus."

All the vertical bars have about the same intensity of black, a characteristic it shares with other members of the species *Symphysodon aequifasciata*. The accompanying color photographs show the actual fish that came from Lago (Lake) Tefé and that were sent to Dr. Schultz to study. The body color has a green tinge but the streaks are definitely green. Most of the colorful hybrid varieties were derived from this subspecies.

While the *Ebenezer* waits in deeper water, I walked ashore to buy fresh fish from the fishermen on Lago Tefé. The people living in Tefé city do not eat discusfish because they are too difficult to catch. The usual food fish are caught with a throw-net.

51

The two discus on this page were caught in different parts of the Tefé area. The Tefé area is large and it includes rivers, lakes and many small streams or igarapes. The discus in this area are very common and each has a slightly different color. They all have a dark red or brown background color, but their stripes vary from light blue to light green. The two Tefé discus shown here are interesting. They both came from the same small branch off Lake Tefé. The light blue one shown on the top of the page was collected in 1974. The darker blue one shown below was collected in 1960. Of course both were photographed in Tefé, but the bottom one had many scales rubbed off its sides and was eventually preserved for further study. The fish on top was brought back alive.

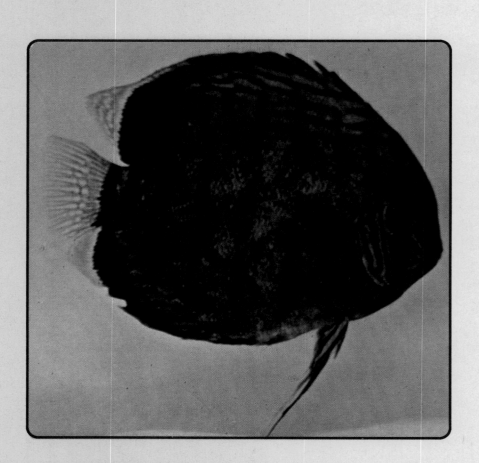

This young indian girl, 14 years old and the mother of three little indians, caught this discus and brought it to me as a gift for the medicine I gave her children. It is an almost totally green discus.

54

Many of the small igarapes feeding the Rio Tefé are un-mapped. I went up this igarape for 3 days in 1974. We paddled by hand, no motor, and found green discus with very green bodies, and many other interesting fishes. The mosquitos were so heavy that sleep was impossible, so we rowed 24 hours day with heavy paddles. I never could bring myself to return without a motorized boat and a mosquito-proof place to sleep. By 1989 when I returned, civilization and its accompanying pollution had wiped out the fish population. What was once everybody's land had now become the property of the local rich man and no one was permitted to fish there without his permission.

The town of Tefé with the re-mains of what was once one of the greatest cities in Brazil. Tefé was a major collecting point for rubber. The indians would bring their balls of semi-processed latex to Tefé to sell to the Portugese traders. The town has been taken over by the Catholic church. The church converted most of the buildings to orphan asylums and religious schools.

This Tefé indian lady
lived far up at the tip of
Lago Tefé. She brought
this discus to me alive.
Of course it died shortly
and was delivered to the
Smithsonian Institution,
but it shows still another
color variation of the
Tefé discus,
*Symphysodon
aequifasciata
aequifasciata.*

56

57

In Lago Tefé, during the rainy season, I would dive and search all possible habitats in which discus might be found. In this submerged old tree trunk I found five baby discus about one inch in diameter.

This is a wild *Symphysodon aequifasciata aequifasciata* from Tefé. It has been thoroughly tamed and fed back to perfect health. In this condition it is suitable for breeding.

These are inbred *Symphysodon aequifasciata aequifasciata*. They do not have the nice red eyes for which the best breeding discus are known.

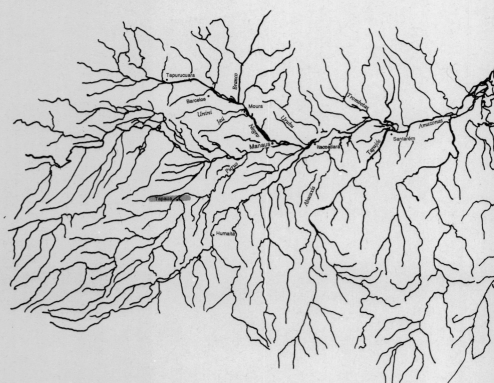

The town of Tapaua on the Rio Purus. The town has only a dozen homes, three of which were vacant. We rented one for $1 per month, but we had to share it with three turtles and two small caimans. In the town we actually found schools of *Cheirodon axelrodi*, the cardinal tetra. The latest scientific designation of the cardinal tetra is *Paracheirodon axelrodi*. In the river we found huge quantities of green discus, *Symphysodon aequifasciata haraldi*. I made this trip with Harald Schultz, and it was based upon the specimens we first collected here that Dr. L. P. Schultz named the fish in honor of Harald Schultz.

61

Scenes along the Rio Tefé. Fires started by lightning destroy most of the Brazilian forests every few years. The blackened trees, which are quickly eaten by insects, disappear in two years.
Discus are never found in areas like these. The reason is that the refuge is not dense enough.

Symphysodon aequifasciata haraldi which I found near Benjamin Constant, Brazil. This is the specimen from which Dr. Leonard P. Schultz described the subspecies, thus this is called the 'holotype'. Essentially, the brown discus, *Symphysodon a. axelrodi*, is brown with almost no blue striping on the body. *Symphysodon a. haraldi* has the top and bottom thirds of its body striped, while *Symphysodon a. aequifasciata* is completely striped.

Symphysodon aequifasciata haraldi Schultz

This subspecies is found throughout the western Amazon. I collected the holotype from which Dr. Schultz described this subspecies at Benjamin Constant, but subsequently it was reported from other areas.

The body color is dark brown with irregular blue streaks running mostly in the upper and lower quarters of the body. For aquarists, the fish can be diagnosed by its light blue streaks and the body being darker than *S. a. aequifasciata*.

Dr. Schultz named this fish in honor of Harald Schultz.

The fish shown on the facing page was a large fish from the far end of the range of *Symphysodon aequifasciata haraldi*. Closer in to the Amazon River is the same subspecies from the Rio Purus. This fish was well acclimated and is shown in its full color under bright light. It is also a wild *Symphysodon aequifasciata aequifasciata*.

The indians help us in fishing. They collect the large vines which, when dried, can be bashed on rocks and shaken into the water to produce a fish poison called *timbo*. It is similar to rotenone. This enables us to catch the fish while they are stunned and before they die. It is only necessary to resort to chemicals when the discus are hiding in the rocks or in dense vegetation and we can't get to them. The indians shown here are carrying pieces of *timbo* root. Timbo fishing is a daytime activity. At night we can use dipnets and strong lights.

The most famous American discus breeder is unquestionably Jack Wattley. Not only is Wattley unique in America, but he is unique worldwide in that he raises his discus artificially. He removes the discus eggs and feeds the young on powdered chicken egg. The fish shown here are the result of various crosses within the genus *Symphysodon aequifasciata*. Many people refer to this color as the 'Wattley Coerulia', but it is just another blue color variety among the so-called royal blue, powder blue, Tarzoo blue, turquoise and just plain blue. The fancier the name, the more expensive the fish!

In 1980 I sailed down the Rio Madeira to a town called Humaita. I fished all around the area and found this wonderful green discus which eventually I ascertained to be *Symphysodon aequifasciata haraldi.* It had the same characteristics as the discusfish from the Rio Purus and it wasn't until I had a map made during the high water time that I discovered that the place where I found the fish, the Rio Ipixuna, was really a tributary of the Rio Purus and not the Rio Madeira even though it was only 45 km from Humaiata which is on the Rio Madeira. Since I only found this one specimen further analysis was impossible. It is possible and likely that this may still be another subspecies of *Symphysodon aequifasciata.*

66

The dark bars in this fish have been bred out of it. The color that is left seems to indicate that it came from basically *Symphysodon aequifasciata* stock.

This specimen is intermediate between a fully colored *Symphysodon aequifasciata aequifasciata* from Tefé and the barless beauty shown on the facing page. Note the metallic appearance of the scales on the lower part of the body. It is this characteristic which was intensified during years of selective breeding and which made the fish on the facing page possible.

The Rio Purus at
Tapaua, home of
*Symphysodon
aequifasciata haraldi.*

In Lago Tefé, the home of the green discus, *Symphysodon aequifasciata aequifasciata,* the author worked out the system of successful discus collection. The fish were stored in large floating nets, like the blue net shown in the photo. Long-handled dip nets (shown on top of the plastic fish box) are used to handle the discus, as well as to catch them at night among the dense vegetation. After a week of collecting several thousand discus, the *Ebenezer* starts to carry the fishes back down the Amazon to Manaus where Adolfo Schwartz has his holding facility. Eventually, the discus end up in Miami at International Fisheries, from where they are shipped worldwide after being conditioned.

The author and the *Ebenezer*, a boat that I have used for more than 35 years of discus collecting. It is fair to say that this boat has carried more than 5 million discusfish.

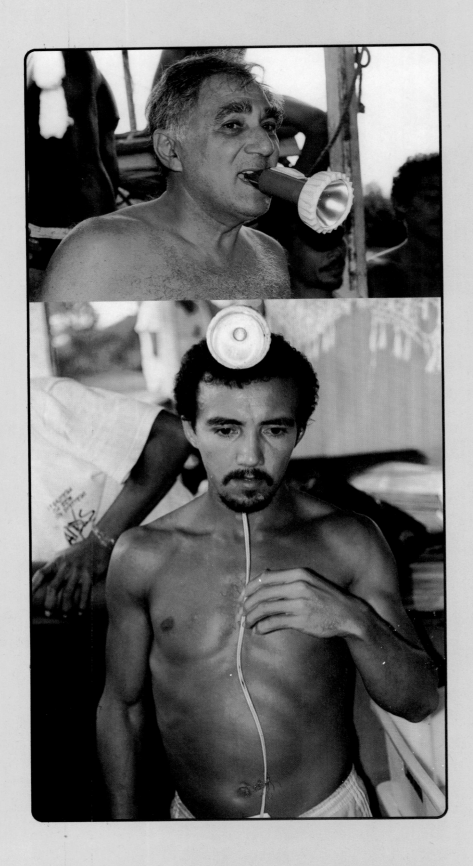

The problem is always finding a strong light that lasts a long time and is easy to handle. Using a car battery, we run a long line to a light affixed to the top of our head, or, alternatively, we put a piece of wood into the end of a flashlight and aim it with our mouth.

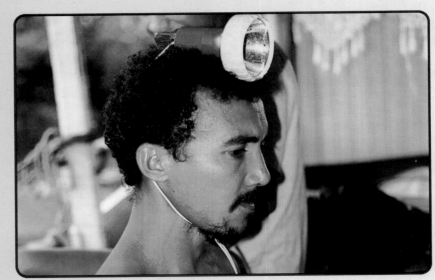

Prior to a discus hunt, we always met at the home of Willi Schwartz. We kept up the tradition. In 1989, before we went to the Rios Jaụ and Unini, we had dinner with Mrs. Willi (Robine) Schwartz and her son Adolfo. Willi had passed away 10 years earlier.

At the Rio Urubu near Itacoatiara in Brazil, I found this brown discus with green stripes. Unfortunately the fish was almost dead when I photographed it, but eventually Dr. Leonard P. Schultz used this particular specimen, from which he described the subspecies *Symphysodon aequifasciata axelrodi*.

The Rio Urubu contained millions of discus in 1960. I went back in 1988 and could not find a single fish.

Symphysodon aequifasciata axelrodi

Schultz

On one of my first discus collecting trips outside the Rio Negro, our boat stopped at the town of Itacoatiara, which is close to the Rio Urubu. "Urubu" means vulture, so this was the river of vultures. We walked about 20 miles along the footpaths which the Indians used, until we reached the river. At that time there were no roads; now you can drive there from Manaus. It took us a day from Manaus by boat to reach Itacoatiara and we were greeted by swarms of mosquitos as we tried to sleep on the boat waiting for daybreak. I went back in 1988 and it was a one hour drive from Manaus.

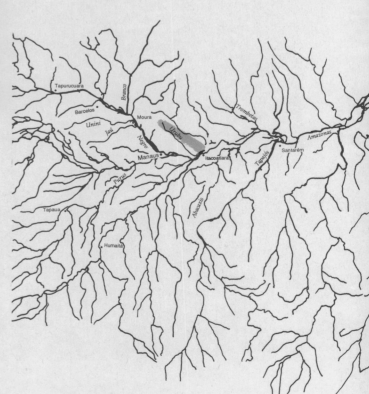

Symphysodon aequifasciata axelrodi

Schultz

This is the hut in which Harald Schultz, our Indian helper, and I lived while studying the fishes of the Rio Urubu. We slept in hammocks and cooked our meals on a wood fire, as shown here. This is a 1960 photo (the author is shown with the helper). In 1988 when I returned, not only was the site developed, but a luxury hotel had been built in this same area and the river had become completely polluted, with only scavengers and a few hardy cichlids like the ubiquitous *Cichlasoma festivum* still present.

Once we reached the Rio Urubu we arranged to rent an Indian hut. We slung our hammocks and went to sleep. Suddenly I was awakened by a fight between some large jaguars. They seemed to be outside our hut. I slowly reached for my rifle (in those days you could bring a rifle into the jungle). Gently, I poked Harald Schultz who was sleeping in a hammock a few feet from me. He stirred and I warned him: "Don't move, Harald. There is a pack of jaguars outside the hut!"

Harald listened for a minute and then started laughing hysterically.

"Those are howler monkeys!" he said.

I couldn't sleep. "Harald, let's go fishing," I said.

Symphysodon aequifasciata haraldi. These are the original wild fish imported into Europe in the 1960-1970 era of discus development.

76

The brown discus, *Symphysodon aequifasciata axelrodi,* has a fairly huge range extending from the area around Belem do Para, near the Atlantic Ocean, over 1,000 miles up the Amazon to the Rio Urubu. This specimen was collected by the author in 1965 in the Belem area (perhaps an 8-hour boat ride out of Belem!). It is the most colorless of all discus. Sometimes I want to hypothesize that the closer one comes to the Atlantic Ocean, the less attractive are the discusfish. This fish was one of the specimens used by Dr. Leonard P. Schultz in his description of the subspecies *axelrodi.*

78

Views of a typical Brazilian trip for discus collecting. All serious commercial discus fishing is done at night. The fishermen's families gather together to gossip while the men are out fishing. Remember, this is the jungle...no television, no radio, no telephone, no lights; during the gathering a single boat is equipped with a lantern and the women and children have their night of social contact. The men have their small dugouts, each equipped with fully charged small batteries with which they power their head lamps (miner's lanterns). As the fishermen return with their catch, they store them in plastic fish boxes and sleep in hammocks on the mothership until all the fishermen arrive. They then get paid for their night's work. Payment is about $10 for 20 adult fish delivered unharmed to the mothership.

Some of the
*Symphysodon
aequifasciata axelrodi*
collected in the Rio
Urubu and acclimated to
an aquarium.

80

We got up and called out to our Indian hosts. They eagerly wanted to help us. We got into a dugout and paddled gently to the other side of the river. On the way we saw hundreds of fishes skimming the surface of the Urubu River. They were searching for insects. Suddenly, without warning, a *Prochilodus* fish jumped into our boat and hit me in the face. I fell overboard into a river laden with piranhas. I was frightened, but again Harald reassured me.

"Piranhas are cowards unless they are starving. They don't attack people. The stories you hear are mostly untrue."

The Indian, whose name was Koorooshira, shot this jaguar with a poisoned arrow. They skinned the jaguar and ate the meat. The hunter who shot the jaguar cut up the meat into large chunks and gave out pieces to each of the women in the village. He kept none for himself.

We crossed the river and found many discusfish hiding among the branches of trees that had fallen into the water as the river washed away the soil holding their roots. We placed a large net around a huge tree, chopped the tree into bits that we could carry, and were rewarded 13 hours later with about a thousand discus. We preserved 75 of them and sent 48 to Dr. Leonard P. Schultz at the Smithsonian Institution. The Indians ate those that were dying; actually we ate some too. The rest we brought back alive to Miami.

When we returned that afternoon, the Indians proudly showed us the huge jaguar they had shot with a poisoned arrow. I looked at Harald and he looked at

81

For almost 40 years I have been collecting aquarium fishes and lecturing about my expeditions. I think that many hobbyists think about collecting fishes in the jungle as a romantic dream. Far from it! The air is filled with mosquitos and other biting insects. The humidity is stifling...and the heat saps your energy. The nights are so cold that you shiver unless covered by two blankets. In the photo, I can be seen at the bow of the boat using a long pole to ascertain the depth of the water. We often were stuck on sand bars. My boat, the *Ebenezer*, was hardly a luxury vessel. The toilet was merely a toilet bowl strategically located over a hole cut in the deck. A tin can was lowered from the window, allowed to fill with water, and then used to flush the toilet. The same was true of the kitchen sink. No running water...only a tin can dropped out of the window and pulled back in filled (hopefully) with water. No refrigeration, radio, television, air conditioning, bath, shower or bed. When we were lucky we slept in hammocks. The crew slept wherever they could, usually on hard boards on top of engines or plastic boxes of fish. The one luxury we had was a portable stove. We brought along bottles of compressed fuel on which the stove operated. These photos, taken in 1988, portrayed a trip up the Rio Negro. Our pilot and surgeon was Dr. Arthur Topilow, who specializes in blood diseases but is an expert sailor, trauma specialist and fisherman.

me. He bought me the jaguar skin to take home. I hung it in my study only to discover I am allergic to cats and had to give the skin away!

Colorwise, *S. a. axelrodi* is the least attractive of the whole species group. It is called the "brown discus" in the fish trade and has the lowest value of all imported discusfishes. Only recently has the fish become desirable since the trade is laden with color varieties (many of which are enhanced with sex hormones) and normal fish are recognized as more reliable breeding stock. The accompanying color photos clearly illustrate this subspecies. The "brown discus" is easily identified by most aquarists.

The fish was named after me by Dr. Schultz because I collected most of the specimens used in the revision of the genus *Symphysodon.*

A brown discus,
*Symphysodon
aequifasciata axelrodi.*
This is a tank-raised
specimen of the type
bred in Hong Kong and
exported worldwide. This
is the least expensive of
the various wild types,
but is basic to most
breeding programs
because the strain is
genetically fixed.

The author, Dr. Herbert R. Axelrod, returning from a night of discus fishing. I use a small dugout, as does every other discus fisherman. Two long-handled small dipnets are used to trap the discus which are blinded by a strong light. The captured discus are then put into an inch or two of water in a plastic fish box, a corner of which can be seen at the lower right edge of the photo.

These are fishes from the Belem area. They are called brown discus, *Symphysodon aequifasciata axelrodi,* in the U.S.A. and Europe, but in Southeast Asia they are sometimes called 'Hong Kong reds.' Discus are very gentle fish and may be kept together without fighting. Spawning pairs become territorial. Discus feel very much at home in heavily planted aquariums, but almost all commercial breeders use tanks which are bare except for the spawning medium, usually a clay pot.

The Japanese people are very partial to discus varieties, as they are to many other fishes, birds and other living forms. They call this color variety of *Symphysodon aequifasciata* the *'Shirase Royal Thunder Flash.'* It has been known in other areas as the Tarzoo blue, the Mack powder blue, the coerulea and the blue turquoise. These are nothing but common names (even if they seem uncommon) and have no scientific value for identification.

HOW DISCUS
REPRODUCE

One of the main reasons that discus
are so attractive as pets is their almost
unique breeding process. Even though
the first discus spawnings took place in
America in the 1930s, produced by a Mr.
Dodd, hardly anyone was able to
duplicate his feats. When Dodd moved
to another house, he could no longer
breed the discus. He claimed that the
water was changed. Who knows.

Over the years more and more discus
spawned, and now, in the 1990s, tank-
raised discus are available everywhere,
and they breed easily if properly fed and
cared for.

What makes discusfish so unique?
Very few fishes have fry which are
'parasitic' on their own parents. This is
true of discus because, I theorize, the
discus originated in the Rio Negro. The
Rio Negro is so highly acid that
practically no infusorians or edible
microorganisms are available as food for
the fry. Thus the fry had to eat the slime
from their parents' bodies. As the discus
migrated down the Rio Negro to the
Amazon and its tributaries, this habit
remained even though it is not necessary
in the usual Amazonian habitats, which
are heavily laden with nutrients and
infusorians. This means (according to my
personal theory only) that the discus
originated in the Rio Negro and they are
still in an active period of evolution.
Thus the many different color varieties.

Interesting questions are opened by
this theory of mine. For instance, if the
discusfish originated in the Rio Negro
and migrated through the Amazon, how
did the Rio Negro species, *Symphysodon
discus*, get to the Rio Trombetas and the
Rio Abacaxis, both of which are widely
separated from the Rio Negro?

Everyone assumes that the Amazon is
the primary river in South America, thus
it was there before the Rio Negro flowed
into it.

How about a theory like this: The Rio
Negro originated where it now begins
but went through Brazil to the Atlantic
Ocean, taking a course which is now
occupied by the Amazon. The Rio Negro
was later joined by the Rio Solimões at
Manaus to form the Amazon, but in the
interim it spread *Symphysodon discus*
throughout its course. When the various
other rivers began feeding into the
Amazonas and it got larger and larger,
different types of discusfish developed
(the *aequifasciata* species) in the richer,
less acid waters of the Solimões/Amazon
system, but those rivers which were not
flooded by the Amazon (such as the Rio
Abacaxis), kept their highly acid black
water and therefore were able to
maintain the original *discus* species and
subspecies. This is the only theory I
know to the explain the appearance of
Symphysodon discus interspersed within
the range of *Symphysodon aequifasciata*.

Knowing this, then, we should strive to select a pair of discus and let them raise their own young. This is most easily accomplished by purchasing a dozen young fish in the color variety which best suits your taste...and pocketbook. These should be placed in the largest possible aquarium, certainly one of at least 50-gallon capacity, and fed well, often and carefully. Do not overfeed. Stay away from tropical fish foods which contain excess heavy metals. Change the water as frequently as possible. A 10% change every day is desirable. When two fish pair off and begin to clean a possible spawning site, isolate the pair into a breeding tank which has been previously prepared and which will serve as the home for this pair forever. The same water and cleanliness are required in this spawning tank as in the community aquarium in which all the potential discus breeders have been raised.

If you are lucky, the pair will spawn within a week. Unfortunately, most of these young breeders eat their own eggs. This is especially true of breeders about a year old. Sometimes they stop egg-eating, but not always. After having devoured their eggs, they seem to be energized to spawn again very quickly, usually within 10 days.

You can leave the pair together for months, perhaps having 3-4 spawns per month if they continue to eat their eggs. Once you have given up on the leave-them-alone policy, you have three alternatives.

First, you can remove the spawn and hatch them artificially. This process is detailed in Jack Wattley's famous discus book. They are then fed with powdered egg until they can take newly hatched brine shrimp. The process of tending to each clutch of eggs and young every 8 hours is tedious.

Second, try to hatch the eggs without the breeders (it's easy) by substituting a heavy stream of air against the eggs and using a water sterilizer like methylene blue or some other dye which your local aquarium shop can supply. When the fry become free-swimming, add them to a school of fry which already exists with less cannibalistic parents.

The third way is the most effective. Build a screen which fits over the eggs (there are photos of these screens in this book). The breeders care for the eggs through the screen but cannot get to them to eat them. The young move through the screen to the parents once they are free-swimming. The fry may still be gobbled up by the parents, but fewer parents eat the babies than eat their own eggs.

During spawning, the female lays 10-20 eggs at a time, until she has laid from 200 to 500. The male fertilizes each clutch as it is deposited. Both parents have a spawning tube protruding from their anal pores during spawning. The female's ovipositor (spawning tube) is thicker than the male's because it must accomodate eggs, which are a lot thicker than the male's sperm.

Spawning usually takes about an hour. The eggs hatch in 56 hours in water at 84 degrees F.

One of Jack Wattley's most magnificent productions has been his fully colored Wattley Coerulea (sometimes spelled *coerulia*). This fish has a long history of inbred *Symphysodon aequifasciata* selections in its developmental history.

COLOR VARIETIES OF HYBRID DISCUS

Discus are closely related to freshwater angelfish of the genus *Pterophyllum*. These fish are also found in South America from Guyana to south of the Amazon River. Angelfish have been bred in several color varieties from solid yellow to solid black. They have also been developed with different finnage. The essential forms have either normal fins or very long fins.

Discus breeders have not as yet been able to raise discus with as elaborate a fin elongation as angelfish, but they have been able to develop more color varieties...and these color varieties are much more interesting than angelfish color varieties.

The established color varieties are as follows:

The **BLUE** discus are found in various intensities of blue from light powder blue to a darker cobalt blue.

The **GREEN** discus are found in various intensities of green from light green to a medium green. There are many more blue varieties than green varieties.

The **RED** variety is really the brown, which is most obvious in *Symphysodon aequifasciata axelrodi*. Recent developments of brown, red, gold, molasses and honey are named, but as once noted, *'beauty is in the eyes of the beholder.'*

The many names given to the many colors are for advertising purposes only. When you buy discus, get the color which best suits you. If you buy discus from a mail order advertisement in a MAJOR aquarium magazine, ask the seller to refer you to a specific color photograph in this or some other discus book so you know exactly what to expect. Unfortunately at least one famous German exporter has been selling to unsuspecting buyers overseas discus which were neither the size nor the color he represented. Buyers beware. The safest place to buy discus is from your local petshop.

96

The father of the fancy discus, Jack Wattley. Mr. Wattley is shown visiting an aquarium shop in Japan in 1988.

This is the fish which made Jack Wattley famous. The Wattley Coerulea is a fish with dark, intense blue on the bottom third of its body and light green in the middle third. An indication that this is an old fish (three years is old) is the nuchal hump which develops on the heads.

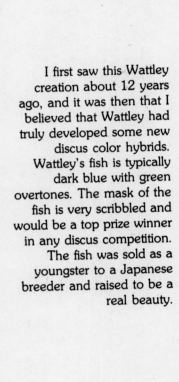

I first saw this Wattley creation about 12 years ago, and it was then that I believed that Wattley had truly developed some new discus color hybrids. Wattley's fish is typically dark blue with green overtones. The mask of the fish is very scribbled and would be a top prize winner in any discus competition. The fish was sold as a youngster to a Japanese breeder and raised to be a real beauty.

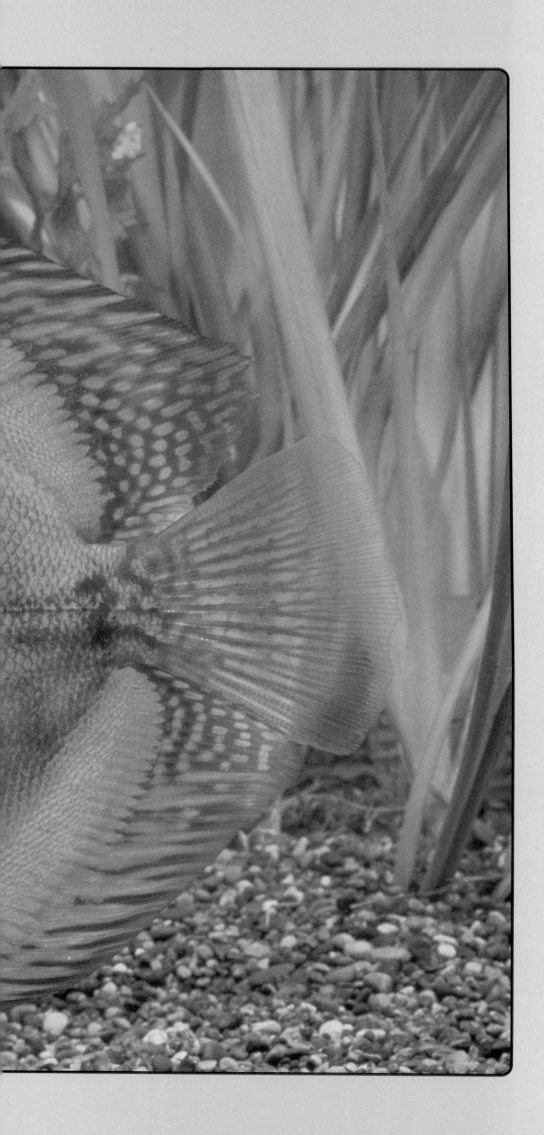

The Wattley solid blue discus. As with most of Wattley's strains, the blue is always accompanied by a slightly green tinge. Wattley was the first breeder in the U.S.A. to produce an almost uniformly colored fish.

101

Dr. Eduard Schmidt-Focke was the discus-breeding genius of Europe. He must certainly be credited with the development of Germany's discus breeding leadership. His most popular invention was the *'Schmidt-Focke Checkerboard Red.'* This is closely similar to the so-called scribbled discus but the blue areas on this strain are non-connected and isolated on the center of the fish's body.

The Oriental discus breeders were not able to get pure strains of either Wattley's discus or Dr. Schmidt-Focke's fish. They had to take what they could find on the so-called second hand market. The Hong Kong breeders developed the high body, hi-fin cobalt turquoise discus. These fish are characterized by the first soft rays of the dorsal being elongated. The ratio of the body height to the body length is about 10% greater than in normal discus. Normal discus have about an equal measurement from the tip of the snout to the end of the caudal peduncle (body length) as compared to the body height. The illustration shows a pair preparing to clean off a clay flowerpot preparatory to spawning.

104

Taiwanese breeders have produced this hi-finned half black discus.

A German brilliant discus variety (that's the name given this fish by Japanese discus lovers) tending her newly deposited eggs. The eggs are just beginning to develop, as indicated by the white polar cap barely visible in this photo.

The female German brilliant on the facing page is being bred with a German cobalt turquoise. These are the names under which these fish are sold in Japan. Each country has its own name for the same fish...and some countries have several names for the same fish, just to make matters that much more confusing.

108

A German brilliant female tending her eggs while her mate, a German cobalt turquoise, awaits further egglaying. This is an interesting photo. Can you find the single fry hatched out? It seems that the pair had spawned a week earlier and eaten all the eggs except one. That egg hatched and the youngster survived by eating the slime off the spawning site. The breeders seem to ignore the little fish.

109

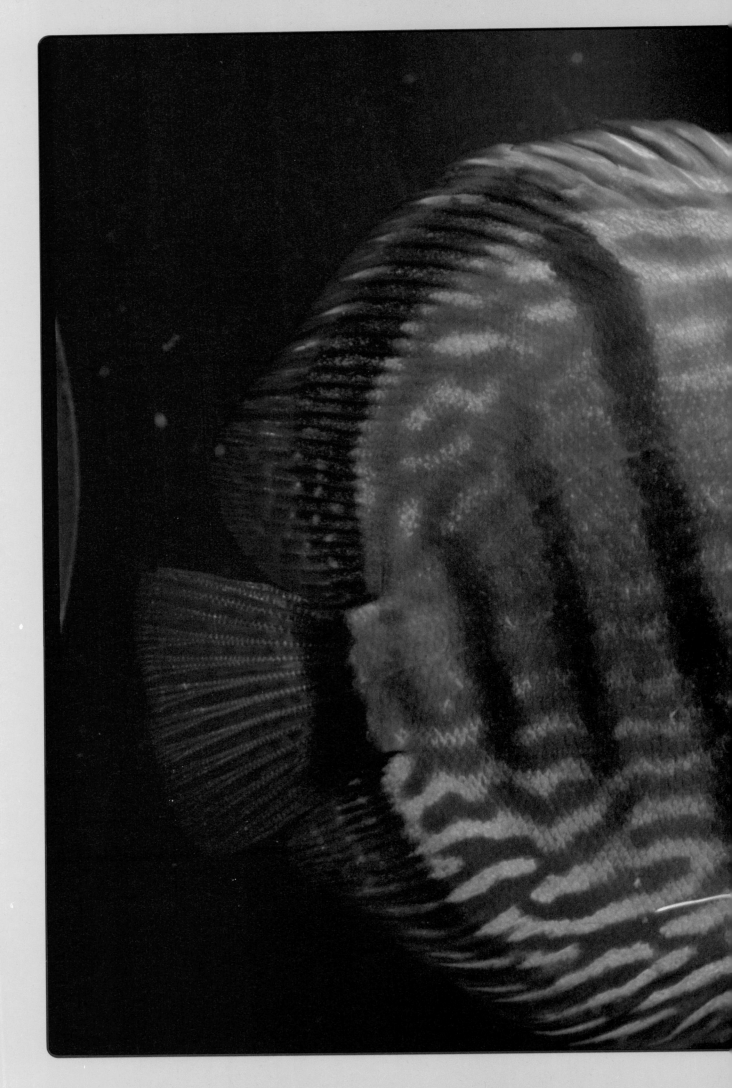

110

This red royal blue is carefully eating the eggs which were not fertilized. Those eggs which turn white have not been fertilized or have died. They must be removed or they will be attacked by fungus (*Saprolegnia*) which might spread and envelop the entire spawn.

112

These are two Wattley hi-fin high bodied fish. They have just seen their eggs become fungused (visible in the background). This is a young pair, and they will spawn again in a week or two.

There are high bodied fish and there are elongated discus, like the pair shown here. These scribbled discus were produced in Japan and they are shown here spawning on a large aquarium plant leaf. The female is awaiting the male, who is fertilizing the eggs just laid. The papilla protruding from the anal pore of each fish is an indication of the sex of the fish. The female's ovipositor is always thicker than the male's papilla.

These are a pair of Yat Sui cobalt turquoise discus. They have spawned, and the eggs were protected from their parents by having a wire cage built around them. Many of the eggs have died before hatching, but luckily they were not attacked by fungus and the healthy eggs hatched out perfectly. As soon as the fry are free-swimming, they will feed from the sides of their parents. Discus parents are more reluctant to eat their living fry than to eat their unhatched eggs.

A closeup view of unhatched discus eggs.

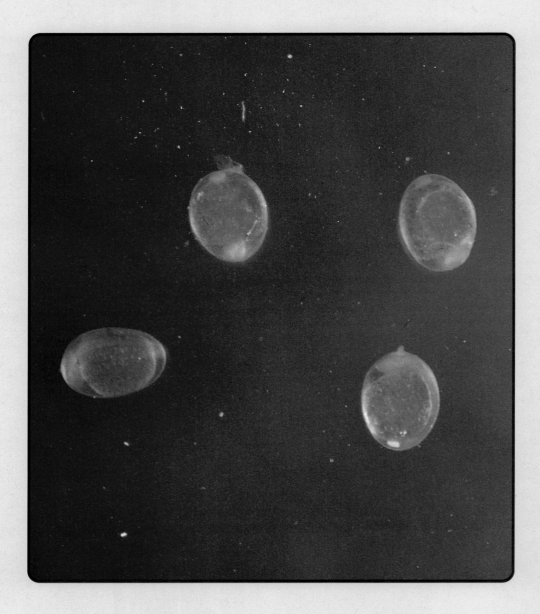

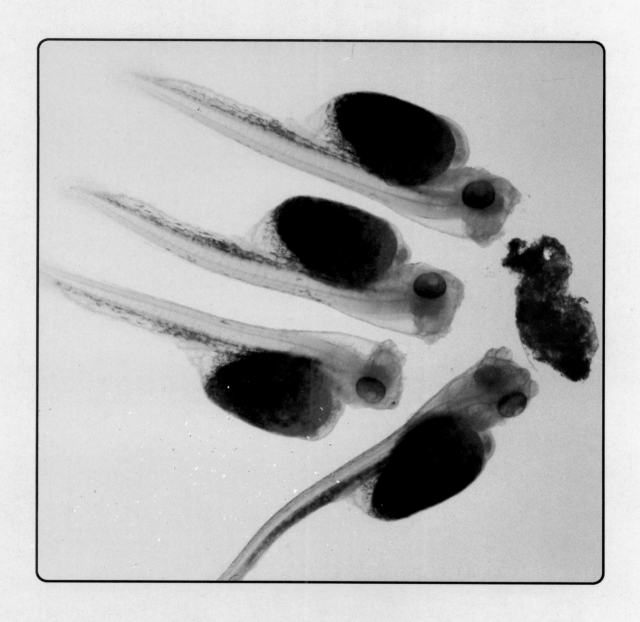

117

About a 12 times
enlaragement of four
newly hatched discus fry.
The rough area around
the head is the glue
gland by which the
discus fry attaches itself
to the spawning site.

118

Symphysodon aequifasciata axelrodi, the brown discus, with 80 of its fry. The fry are 'parasitic' on the parents and eat slime from their parents' bodies until they are almost one month old. This is an interesting photo because it is a very rare sight that discus fry eat perpendicular to the feeding surface. The mouth of discus fry is under the head and not straight out as in the adult. Most breeders allow the fry to feed from the slime covering the adult fish. Others, like Jack Wattley, hatch the eggs in a heavily aerated, deeply medicated (methylene blue) hatching tank and raise the resulting fry artificially using powdered chicken egg yolk. This technique enables Wattley to produce many more discus than others in a much smaller space.

121

A full color turquoise with some of her young feeding from her body slime.

125

A brown discus,
*Symphysodon
aequifasciata axelrodi*,
with her fry which are
about 25 days old. They
are almost ready to be
weaned to newly
hatched brine shrimp.

Perhaps Jack Wattley's greatest contribution to the hobby of keeping and breeding fancy discusfish was his development of a technique for the hatching, rearing and feeding of baby discus without the assistance of their parents. Why was this such a great feat?

Discus are unusually fond of eating their own eggs. It would be a fair guess 95% of the freshly imported discus of the 1960s would eat their own eggs...if you could ever get them to spawn! It was only after many attempts by many breeders that tank-raised discus were available in large enough quantities for professional breeders to become involved. Today, discus breeding is big business, with millions of tank-raised discus young being sold worldwide. The solution to egg-eating by discus breeding pairs took many avenues. The Asian breeders built wire cages around the spawning site and successfully raised the eggs within sight of the breeders. The breeders would blow water onto the eggs and keep the eggs healthy. Once the eggs hatched and the young became free-swimming, they would go to their parents and feed from the parents' slime covering. In cases like this about 60% of the hatch survived as the unfertilized or dead eggs would fungus and the fungus often spread to the rest of the eggs.

It is no trick to remove the eggs from the aquarium once they have been laid and fertilized. The only problem is to feed the young once they are free-swimming. Probably originating in the Rio Negro, discus had problems. The Rio Negro is so acid and so sterile that it is nothing more than dirty distilled water. In such water microorganisms can hardly survive and baby fishes cannot feed on their usual fare. Only during the rainy season (January through May) can most of the fishes of the Rio Negro spawn and the fry successfully feed on natural microorganisms. This is due to the rather huge rise in the Rio Negro during the rainy season. In January or February the Rio Negro overflows its banks and covers the ground surrounding it to a depth of many feet. The small fish spawn on the submerged grasses and the young eat the resulting infusoria as well as ants and other small insects trapped by the rising waters. Larger fish spawn in the river and their fry eat the smaller fry. Discus fry, however, stay with their parents...and their parents do not move very far from their hideouts in deep water at the roots of dense vegetation. Thus the fry of discus had to evolve by feeding on their own parents. During the spawning cycle the slime covering on the parent discus becomes thicker. The fry eat that. Analysis of this slime indicated it was high in protein and fat, about 80% protein and 3% fat. Egg yolk has very high protein and fat (and lots of cholesterol, which the young fish need). But powdered egg yolk merely floats on top of the water when sprinkled. It took Wattley and a few other pioneers but a short time to figure out how to do it. They added water to the egg powder, then smeared the edge of a soup plate with the sticky egg powder mash. The fry were added to the soup plate along with some of their own aquarium water and they fed easily on the inclined sides of the plate. The photos I made at Wattley's hatchery show clearly how successful this technique is. After each feeding, the plate is cleaned and 8 hours later the routine starts again. A discus hatchery is really a *hatchery*.

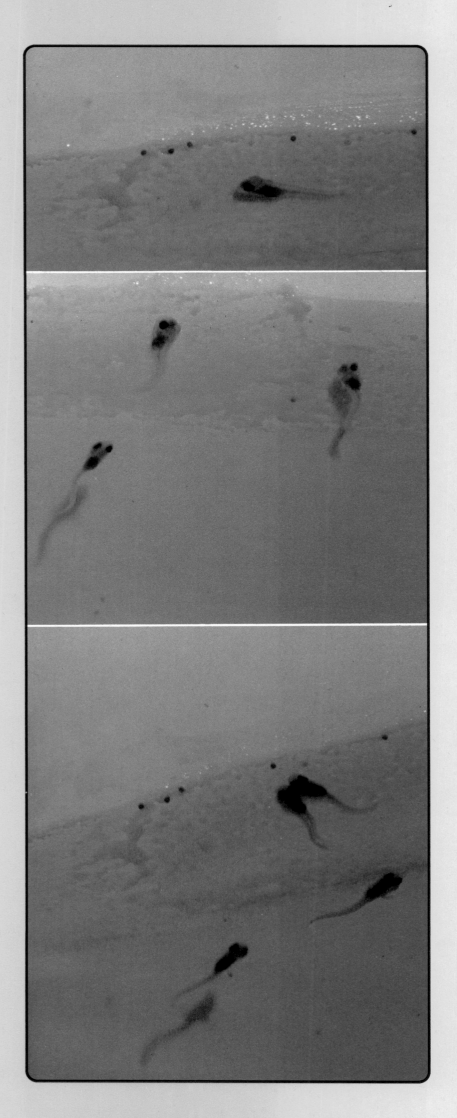

This German brilliant cobalt was previously considered as the ultimate in discus breeders' art. The body is almost totally covered with intense and attractive cobalt blue. The fins are long and held erect. The few body spots, though detrimental from a show standard point of view, make an interesting relief.

128

Inbred hybrids of selected *Symphysodon aequifasciata* from the Purus River and the Tefé region. The *haraldi* has the center part of its body lacking the color of the *S. a. aequifasciata*, but when these two subspecies are crossed many unpredictable results may be expected. Not only do these young fish show excellent color, but their body form is superb. The fins are very high, held erect and exceptionally long and colorful. Discus body form has now become a breeding objective.

When discus are kept in an aquarium with a low level of lighting, they are much more at ease. In their natural habitat they stay in the shadows about midwater between the top and bottom layers. Here we have a pair of *Symphysodon aequifasciata.* The colorful specimen is from Tefé and is *S. a. aequifasciata;* the brown discus is from the lower Amazon south of Manaus and is *Symphysodon a. axelrodi.* Notice their long their pelvic fins.

A closeup of a pair of *aequifasciata*. The highly colored fish in the foreground is a female *Symphysodon aequifasciata aequifasciata* from the Tefé region of Brazil. The discusfish in the background is *Symphysodon aequifasciata haraldi* from the Rio Purus. Both of these fish were imported from Brazil as young fish and were conditioned and raised in an aquarium. Breeders are continually experimenting with cross breeding various subspecies and hybrid varieties to produce more spectacular offspring.

In 1965 I collected this spectacular fish in the Tefé region. Highly colored dominant males like this one were very rare. Perhaps one fish in a hundred was so highly colored. The reason for this intensity of color was never satisfactorily explained since dominance usually has meaning only in fishes which school. Discus, once they can feed themselves, leave their parents and live in isolation until they find a mate. I sold these fish to Europe (through Gulf Fish Farms, which I owned at that time). By breeding this fish with other highly colored females, the beginning of the so-called *turquoise* strain of discus was born. Only fish of the species *Symphysodon aequifasciata* were involved in the development of the early turquoise strains.

Early pioneers in
Switzerland produced a
hi-fin, high body form of
turquoise in the 1970s.
These two fish
characterize the best that
was available during
those years. Eventually
these turquoise became
the basis for the scribbled
or checkerboard pattern.
They have unusually
high dorsal and anal fins.

While the Europeans were striving for a deep cobalt and turquoise blue discus, the Asiatic breeders were going for powder blue, metallic fish like the two shown here. Body forms like the high form in the top fish contrasted nicely with the elongated form in the bottom fish. Normally, discusfish have a body height equal to body length.

The ultimate goal of every animal breeder, including breeders of discusfish, is to establish a strain which reproduces genetically pure individuals all of whom look alike. This goal has been achieved in Japan with the strain the Japanese call 'Red Royal Blue Discus.' This is a view of some 3-month-old discusfish of that strain. The genetic basis of these fish is the early European turquoise discus.

Red royal blue discus like this one are being produced in Thailand.

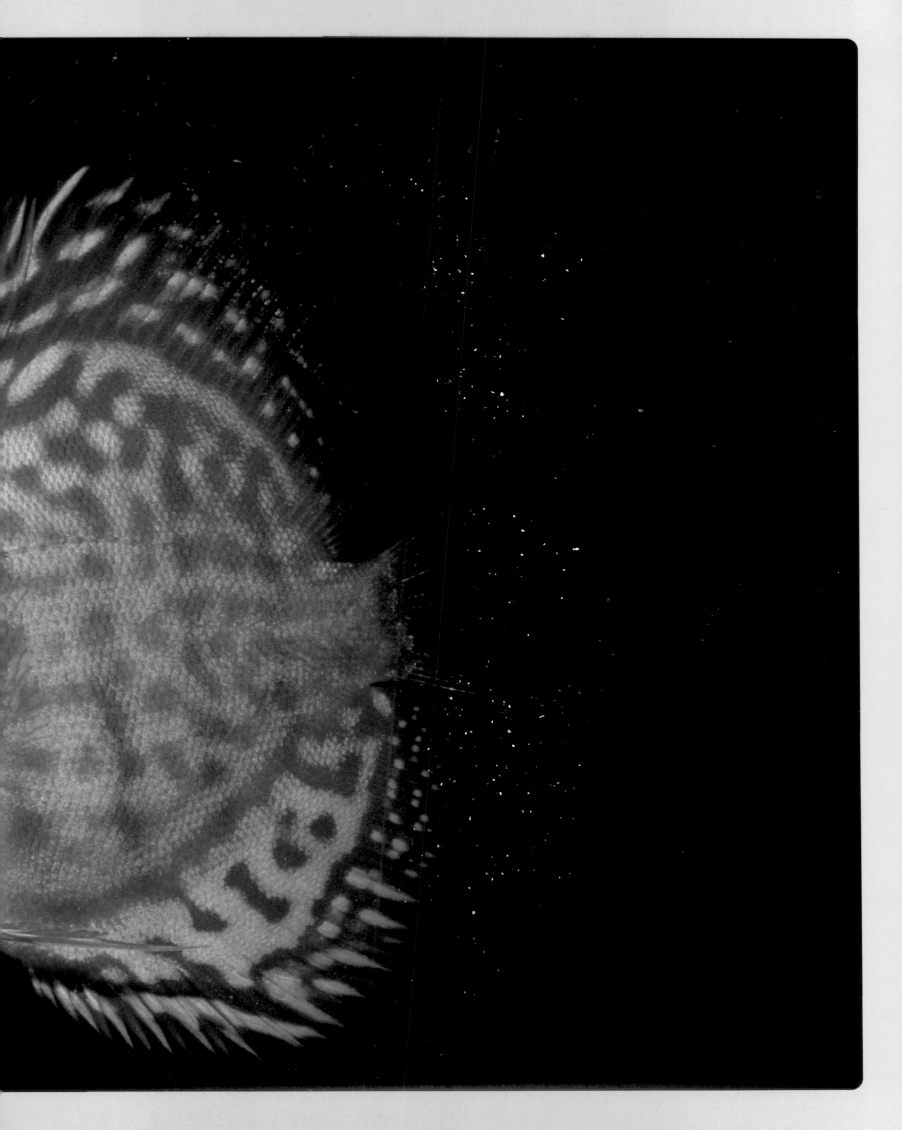

New strains are appearing in Southeast Asia. More and more yellows, with elongated soft dorsal fin rays and high body forms seem to be an Asiatic specialty.

As the discus in Singapore and Malaya become inbred for the powder blue color, the amount of red or brown decreases or disappears. Compare the fish in the photo at bottom left to the fish in the photo at right and you can easily see the disappearance of the red or brown.

140

In 1988 Asian breeders were able to produce metallic discus with powder blue, turquoise green and red markings, as evidenced by these two fish. These champion fish were entered into a discus competition organized in 1989 in Singapore, where I was a judge. That week of judging experience enabled me to photograph almost all the discus varieties and to speak with breeders from all over the world. Interestingly, the German discus entered into the show were eliminated in the first round of judging.

The red royal blue
discus developed in
Thailand.

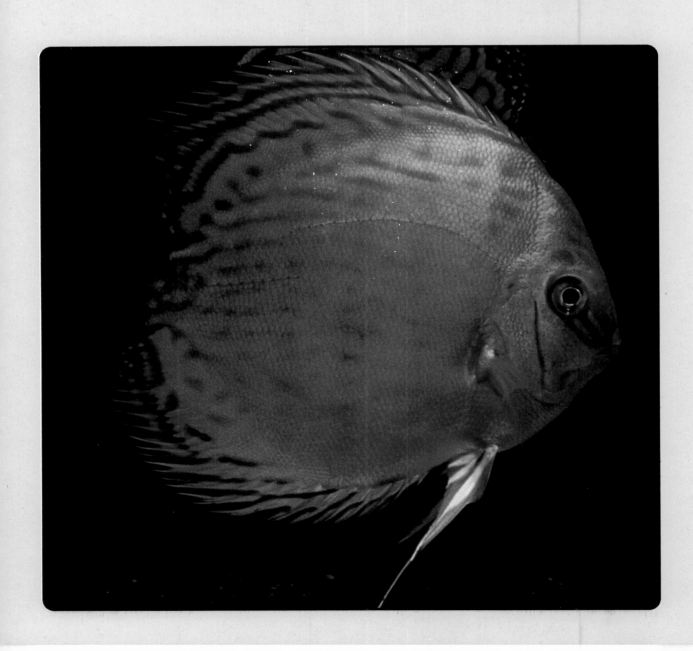

A green turquoise, full
color discus from
Asian breeding. Now
that so many blue
varieties are available,
professional breeders
are striving to produce
a green fish.

This is the so-called *'Royal Green'* discus from Japan. It was produced by crossing a wild *Symphysodon aequifasciata aequifasciata* from Tefé with the Japanese red royal blue discus. You need a vivid imagination to understand why this fish is called 'green.'

144

In Japan this fish is being sold as
a wild *Symphysodon
aequifasciata haraldi*. However,
that is doubtful. The fish is much
more highly colored than *haraldi*
and is probably *Symphysodon
aequifasciata aequifasciata.*

The expert Japanese
breeder and
photographer Fumitoshi
Mori is succesfully
inbreeding the red royal
blue discus which has an
elongated body shape.
He is the Japanese
leader in discus
production...perhaps
the Wattley or Schmidt-
Focke of Japan!

Red royal blue discus spawning.

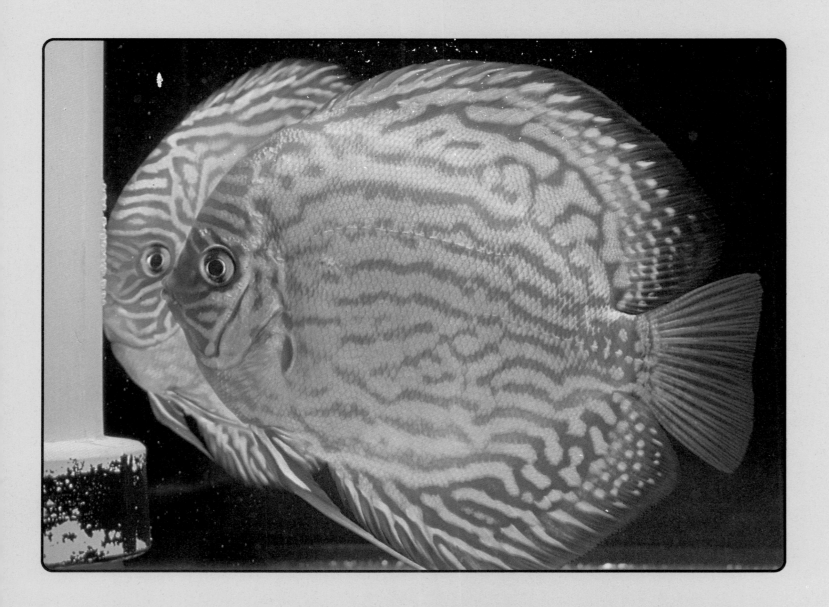

The red royal blue discus
from Thailand. These
fish are being inbred; a
school of their young is
shown on the facing
page.

This is a school of very similar offspring
of the fish shown on the facing page.
These red royal blues, as they are
called in Japan, are considered a fixed
strain.

Hong Kong breeders first developed this full color turquoise from stock originating in Germany. By careful inbreeding it became the basis for the so-called scribbled discus. Highly scribbled discus were developed by Dr. Eduard Schmidt-Focke, a German medical doctor who had a lifelong hobby of breeding Siamese fighting fish and discus. Dr. Schmidt-Focke called his strain of scribbled discus *'checkerboard discus.'*

The scribbled discus
produced in Asia.

The scribbled discus
derived from the original
Dr. Schmidt-Focke
strain.

Two scribbled discus developed in Southeast Asia. The scribbled discus seem to grow larger than ordinary discus because of the phenomenon known as *'hybrid vigor.'*

The Japanese breeder
Tetsuo Harado perfected
this strain which he calls
the *'Hi-fin Morpho
Turquoise.'*

153

This is the ideal German
brilliant turquoise so
highly prized in Asia
during 1990 as basic
breeding stock.

Japanese domestic
discus called the
'Japanese Turquoise' in
Japan. It was produced
by the discus breeder
named M. Abe.

This was the 1989
champion hi-fin scribbled
discus as judged by the
author in Singapore. The
long trailing dorsal fin
rays were twice as long
as those of the nearest
competitor. The fish had
to be raised in solitary
confinement so the long
doral rays would not be
chewed off by other fish.

A matched pair of red-
eyed hi-fin, high body
form German brilliant
turquoise discus
produced from Degen
stock. The redder the
eye, the more valuable
the strain.

The ideal green turquoise
discusfish.

The Japanese breeder
Shuichi Fude produced
the cobalt turquoise
discus.

The famous Japanese
red strain of turquoise.
These fish have very
long pelvic fins.

A German brilliant, fully
colored turquoise.

162

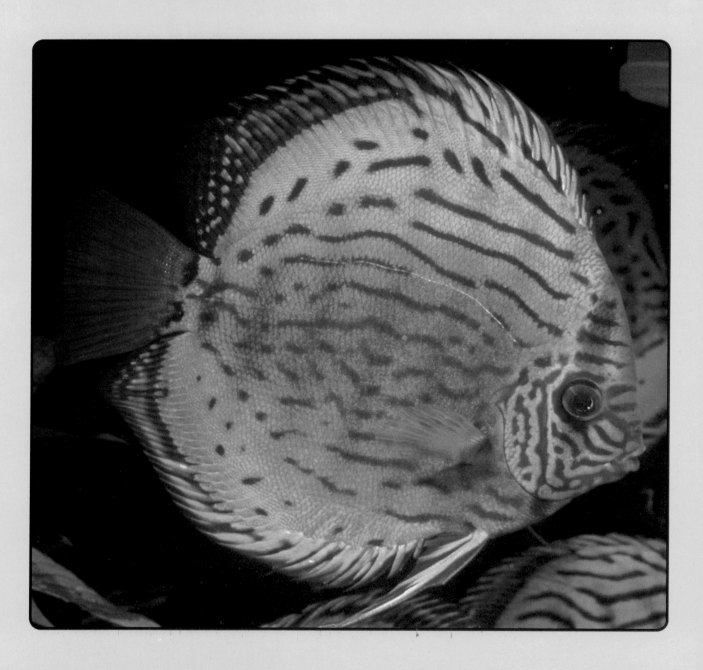

163

A Hong Kong fully
colored turquoise.

Black-barred German
brilliant turquoise discus.

Asiatic cobalt turquoise discus.

166

A German cobalt
turquoise discus.

German brilliant discus
raised in Taiwan.

Hong Kong brilliant
turquoise discus.

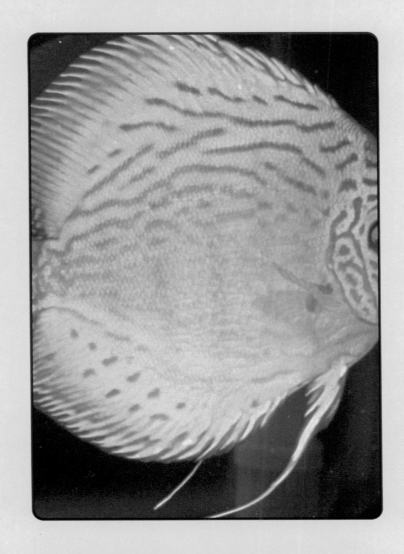

If you look closely at the scales of the Hong Kong brilliant turquoise, you can notice that the scales in the middle body area are only highlighted with pigment and not fully pigmented.

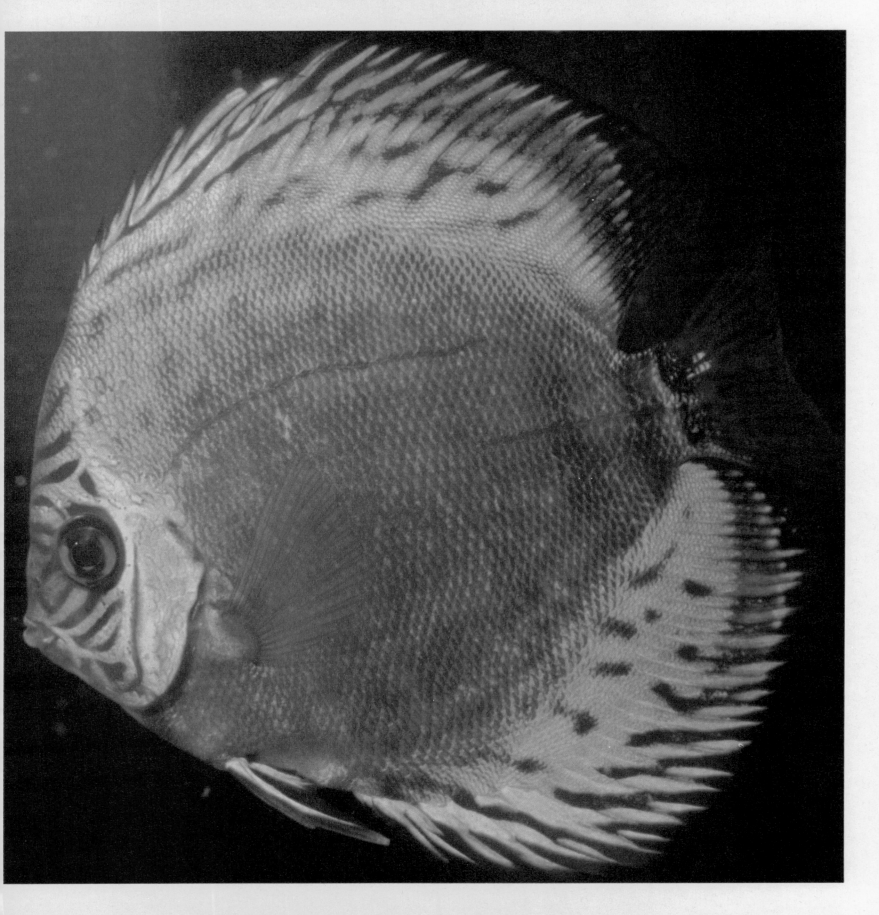

172

Female turquoise discus.

173

Male cobalt turquoise.

174

175

Full color turquoise
discus.

German brilliant
turquoise discus.

Oriental cobalt turquoise
discus.

German brilliant cobalt
discus.

Singapore hi-fin, cobalt
turquoise.

Malayan fully colored hi-
fin cobalt turquoise
discus.

The author, Dr. Herbert R. Axelrod (left), with Dr. Eduard Schmidt-Focke, 1989.

182

This is a fully colored turquoise developed by Dr. Schmidt-Focke.

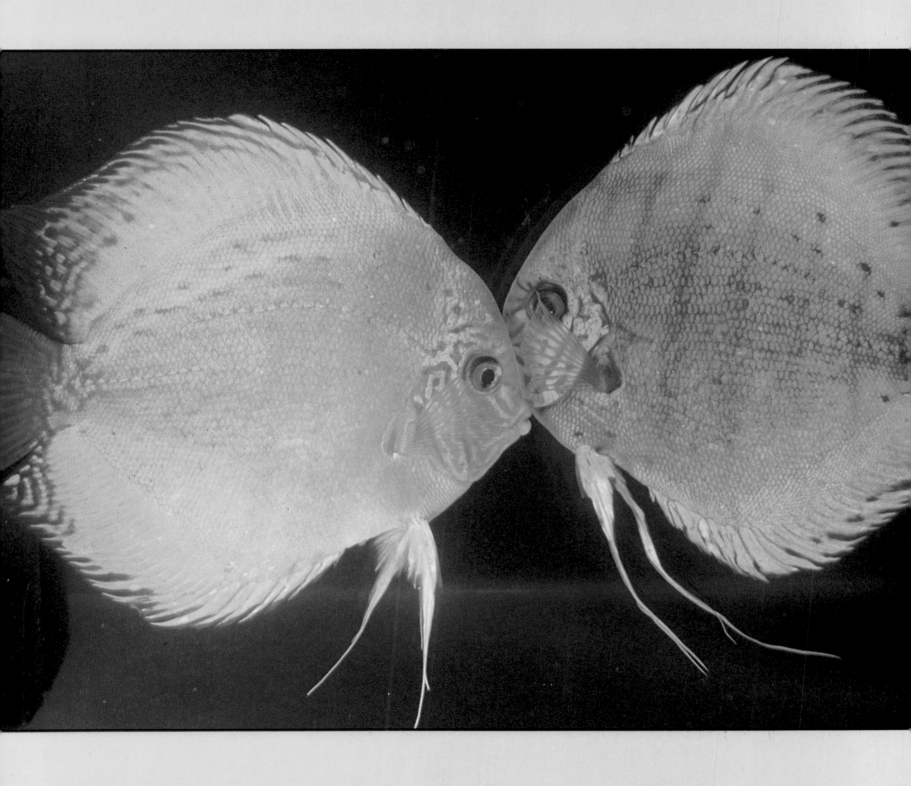

It took Dr. Schmidt-Focke almost 20 years to develop what he calls his *'cobalt turquoise'*. His objective is to breed out the barred pattern, but this is very difficult to do as these marks are usually fright patterns, breeding patterns and age patterns.

185

The cream of the crop...the Japanese Shirase royal thunder!

German cobalt
turquoise.

While Japan, Germany and the U.S.A. are heading for highly colorful cobalt turquoise stocks, the Southeast Asians are striving for lighter powder blues and light greens with metallic sheens.

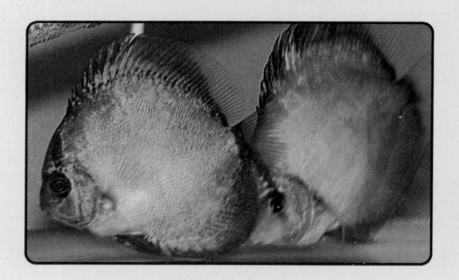

Malaysian discus breeders have produced unbarred discus. They have not proven to be very valuable from a commercial point of view.

188

The goal has been reached for the production of discus without bars! These Malaysian discus shocked the fish world when a tank full were put on display at a fish show in Japan. Unfortunately they were not a commercial success, merely a novelty for discus breeders who want to experiment with them.

IT ALL STARTED WITH THE WILD BROWN DISCUS FROM BRAZIL. The first discus to be spawned in the Far East was the brown discus (they call it the red discus), *Symphysodon aequifasciata axelrodi.* Soon (1972-1990) this form dropped out of vogue as hobbyists went for the turquoise, cobalts and powder blue color forms. Now these wild brown discus from the Belem area are becoming more popular. No longer are they called red or brown. Now they are referred to as *'golden brown'* and *'molasses.'* Molasses is a product of sugar refining. It is the molten sugar before it crystallizes. The word and process, by the way, come from the Brazilian Portuguese word *melaço.*

Index

Photography

In addition to the photos of Fumitoshi Mori, which form the bulk of the photos to be found in this book, photos by the following photographers also grace the pages of *The Allure of Discus*.

Dr. Herbert R. Axelrod; Heiko Bleher; Dr. Martin M. Brittan; Dr. Clifford Chan; the archives of Bernd Degen; Burkhard Kahl; *Midori Shobo,* Japanese fish magazine; H. J. Richter; Fred Rosenzweig; Harald Schultz; Heiner Stolz; A. van den Nieuwenhuizen. Our thanks also to Gan Kian Leng and Gan Khian Tiong for making their beautiful discus available for photography.